BEHIND BARS

Photography by
Grace L. Wojda

Text by
Raymond G. Wojda
Norman Erik Smith
Richard K. Jones

BEHIND BARS

Photography by
Grace L. Wojda

Text by
**Raymond G. Wojda
Norman Erik Smith
Richard K. Jones**

FRONT ENTRANCE: Lebanon Correctional Institution

Director of Communications and Publications: Patricia L. Poupore
Publications Managing Editor: Elizabeth L. Watts
Assistant Editor: Marie G. Unger
Book design: Ralph Butler

Printed in the U.S.A. by St. Mary's Press, Waldorf, MD.

ISBN 0-929310-53-5

Dedication

This book is for our children.

Acknowledgements

Our thanks to William H. Dallman, Warden, Lebanon Correctional Institution, Lebanon, Ohio, for his cooperation with this project. Our thanks also to the officers and inmates who granted us permission for interviews and/or photographs.

To Bettina Gregory and Juan Williams, we express our deepest gratitude for their inspiration and encouragement when we first began our venture.

Special thanks is due Neil Thorburn, President of Wilmington College, Wilmington, Ohio, for his support of this project from conception to completion.

Foreword

Although there are over three-quarters of a million men and women in correctional institutions across the United States, most Americans have never been inside a prison. What they think they know about prisons is what they've seen in movies and on TV—dramatized and simplified versions of the real, complex world of the American prison.

To understand the situation in American prisons, the public needs to see what one is really like; however, the average citizen can't just go to a prison, so the American Correctional Association, through this photo essay, brings the prison to you. You get to see more than just cells—the dining hall, recreation areas, medical facilities, classrooms, work programs, and the visiting room—every aspect of a typical day at a maximum security prison is presented. And you get to hear the truth from correctional officers and inmates about what life is really like on the inside.

As the national membership association for corrections professionals, the ACA works to promote a better understanding of the men and women who live and work in America's prisons. We think *Behind Bars,* through its strong visual images and no-nonsense language, will help us do just that.

Anthony P. Travisono
Executive Director
American Correctional Association

Contents

Introduction

The image most Americans have of a prison is one of violence and brutality, with pot-bellied officers in mirrored glasses and convicts with six-inch scars running across their cheeks. My own work in prisons over the past 13 years, however, has taught me that the prison seldom lives up to these stereotypes. Unfortunately, it has always been difficult to convince others of this. I have often felt that what was needed was a collection of photographs that would accurately and humanely portray prison life, and perhaps break down these negative stereotypes.

This is why I asked Grace L. Wojda if she would be interested in putting such a photographic record together. I knew it would be interesting to see how an accomplished woman photographer captured this "man's world." Furthermore, I had seen her work on the homeless and I was impressed by the dignity she captured in her subjects. I was hoping she would discover that same dignity at the Lebanon Correctional Institution.

I'm pleased to say that she has. Rather than dwell on the oddballs and freaks who inhabit the prison, she has produced a collection of photographs that allows the outsider to catch a glimpse of the everyday reality of the prison. Her photographs capture the loneliness, monotony, apprehensions, fears, and emotions of prison life.

Since Wojda's photographs speak so clearly, we felt it would be best to limit the text and allow the pictures to do the talking. Where words seemed necessary, we chose to use those of the subjects, taken from extensive interviews over a two-year period. The result is a realistic portrayal of life in a close security institution.

Norman Erik Smith, Ph.D.

Welcome to Lebanon

The clanging of the metal doors to the main entrance of the Lebanon Correctional Institution in Lebanon, Ohio, is unlike any sound you have ever heard. It is loud, heavy, and harsh. An exclamation point hammering home the fact that you are now inside a prison.

Suddenly, the placid southwestern Ohio cornfields that surround the prison seem light years away. More than the miles of razor-sharp concertina wire that surround the institution, more than the guard towers that loom over the compound, it is the clanging of the three-inch thick steel doors that defines what life is like inside the prison.

After the first door slides shut, a second door opens and you proceed to the next section, where the officer on duty checks your identification badge and hand stamp. A third door opens and you step into the north corridor. Several inmates are mopping the hallway. Others, clerks for the correctional officers, sit in groups of two or three and sip coffee.

As you pass Central Control and turn down the west corridor, the activity picks up. Some inmates head for their work stations, while others are on their way to the yard for an afternoon of recreation.

You keep looking for comic book stereotypes, but you don't find any. Dressed in prison blues, the inmates come in all shapes and sizes. Some are neatly attired, others are rather sloppy in appearance. There's a certain tough-guy swagger to the way most of them walk, and the language is a tad rougher than what you would hear in a corporate boardroom, but for the most part the inmates look like a cross section of American men.

In some respects, your first view of Lebanon is disappointing. There's no shoving and pushing going on. Nobody is manacled. The inmates don't march in lock step; the officers don't even carry guns. In fact, it all seems pretty tame.

Notice: For security reasons, the names of inmates and officers have been changed.

MAIN GATE: *"Dedicated to the Mending of Lives" is the slogan on Lebanon's main gate.*

But a senior correctional officer quickly puts things into focus.

"This is not a boys' camp," he says. "You never forget what they're here for."

Adds another veteran officer, "You can't totally relax in here. If you do, you're a fool."

The facts would seem to bear him out. Lebanon is a close security prison*, and approximately two-thirds of the inmates are incarcerated for violent crimes. Over 300 of them are serving some form of life sentence, and about 500 are convicted sex offenders.

Lebanon is one of the larger facilities in the state. A single structure, it encompasses 22 acres under one roof. When the prison opened in 1960, it was designed to house 1,300 inmates, but the 1990 census was over 2,000.

The crowded conditions are the result of an explosion of inmates in the state over the past 14 years. In 1976 there were six prisons in Ohio with a total population of about 10,000 inmates. Today, there are 26 prisons, and the total population is now more than 30,000 inmates.

As you continue down the west corridor, you notice a constant hum of voices. An omnipresent sound that infiltrates every portion of the institution, it is the result of 2,000 inmates, 435 employees, and an endless stream of activities under a single roof.

*in between maximum and medium security

As you near the cellblocks the hum grows louder. After just a few minutes, you realize that, in the daytime at least, there is no such thing as peace and quiet at the Lebanon Correctional Institution.

"I don't notice the noise," says one of the officers. "The noise is normal. When it suddenly gets quiet, that's when I start worrying. When it gets quiet, it means that something is about to go down."

OFFICER AT MAIN ENTRANCE: Officers inside the prison do not carry guns. They do, however, carry a PR-24, a plastic baton.

CELL BLOCK, EARLY MORNING: *Because of crowded conditions, most inmates must share a cell. This man has his own cell.*

CELL BLOCK WALL: *The artwork in the cell blocks, as well as the cafeteria and other locations, was done by an inmate.*

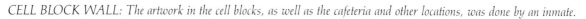

KEY ROOM: All employees and visitors to the prison must pass in front of the key room to have their identification checked.

SHIFT CAPTAIN: Lebanon employs 215 correctional officers.

CELL BLOCK A: A typical cell block has three tiers, or ranges, on each side. Each range holds about 50 cells, for a total of 300 cells per block.

Opposite Page—*JAILBIRD: Birds often land on the concertina wire that surrounds Lebanon. When they touch the ground, they often set off the alarms and officers must make a visual check to ensure that an inmate is not trying to escape.*

2

Close Security

Tuesday is laundry day at Lebanon. In the space of 35 minutes, all 2,000 inmates walk the length of the prison, deposit their old sheets and pillowcases in large hampers, pick up clean linen, and head back to their cells. It is the single biggest mass movement among the inmates that takes place at Lebanon, and it presents its own set of security problems.

During the exchange, the inmates are required—as always—to walk along the right-hand wall. Smoking is not permitted during the exchange because of the danger of someone dropping a lighted cigarette into one of the hampers. The sheets are supposed to be folded and placed over the left shoulder, allowing the officers to watch the inmates' hands and ensure that no weapons or contraband are being transported.

The most obvious security problem, however, is the simple fact that 2,000 inmates are in one place at one time. That's a lot of men to watch and the potential for violence is acute.

In a Hollywood version of such an endeavor, the officers would stand guard with guns and there would be a lot of pushing and shoving going on. Maybe a couple of fights would break out.

But at Lebanon, none of the officers inside the prison carry guns. Only the officers in the towers and those on perimeter patrol—both located outside the compound—are issued firearms.

"All 435 employees, including secretaries and office personnel, are trained in the use of firearms," says a senior officer. "And if there were an extreme emergency, such as a riot, escape attempt, or some sort of attack from the outside, each of these people could be issued a firearm. But in the normal course of events, no one inside the institution carries a gun."

LAUNDRY DAY: Once a week, 2,000 inmates must exchange their linen within a 35-minute period. Inmates are supposed to carry their sheets over their left shoulders.

The day-to-day security rests in the hands of 215 correctional officers. Each officer is issued a set of handcuffs and a PR-24, a plastic or aluminum baton. In addition, the "front line" officers—those who work in the blocks, the hallways, and the shops—carry a "man down" alarm system. The device, worn on the shirt, looks like a radio microphone and sounds an alarm at Central Control if the officer is doubled over or knocked down. The officer can also activate the alarm by pushing a button.

Should an alarm go off in Central Control, the officers manning the station can look at a diagram of the prison, pinpoint where the officer is located, and issue a "Code One" that will in turn send other officers to his assistance. The Central Control officers can also push buttons that will close doors and gates and instantaneously seal off parts of the prison.

One officer estimates that a Code One goes into effect about twice a week. "You would think that a close security institution—where you've got the whole rotten apple combined under one roof—you'd think I'd fight every day. That's wrong. Ten years, actual force? Thirty times. I'm not saying I'm taking out my stick and breaking bones and knocking out teeth. I'm talking about physically restraining somebody.

"I think the worst conflict that I've even come into here was where an inmate turned on me when I had him on the wall and he stabbed me."

The officer further explains that Code One does not necessarily mean an officer is being assaulted. "Here's two inmates fighting. They hear the Code One over the intercom and they start thinking, 'We need to get this over with quick, because any second there's going to be about 20 officers rushing in here.'

"And when they see officers running in, they'll go to their neutral corners, and that's about the extent of things."

Adds another officer, "There's probably less fights in here than at the local schoolyard."

There have been only three murders inside the prison since the institution opened 30 years ago. All three of them were stabbings.

Inmates and officers alike agree that most of the violence that takes place inside the prison is the result of homosexual encounters. "Most of the time it's lover's quarrels," says one inmate. "You stay away from the stuff, you won't have much problem."

Successful escapes from Lebanon are even more rare. No escapes have taken place in the last 12 years, and Lebanon is one of the only prisons its size that can make that claim.

Should anyone attempt to escape and set off an alarm, a signal would sound in Central Control and an order would be issued to respond.

CENTRAL CONTROL: From this room officers can close doors and gates that will instantaneously seal off parts of the prison. All alarms and officers' calls for assistance are also relayed to the control room.

OPI: Ohio Penal Industries makes license plates, beds, and other products. Each inmate is carefully checked by an officer before entering and leaving the work area.

As it is on the outside, drugs are a major problem. Sometimes inmates will smuggle drugs in from other institutions by putting them in a balloon and swallowing it, or by stuffing the drugs up their nose or rectum.

But most of the drugs are brought in by friends and relatives. A urinalysis is given to anyone suspected of being a drug user, and random testing is expected to begin in the near future.

Another big concern of the officers is the possession and use of weapons. Although many inmates maintain that Lebanon is much safer than other institutions and that far fewer weapons exist here than at other places, they do exist.

"We probably find a couple a week," says one officer. "And that ranges from something simple like a bar of soap in a sock to a shank [homemade knife]."

Other contraband items the officers watch for are homemade tattoo guns, stingers (metal objects which can be plugged into the wall to heat a cup of coffee), and gambling paraphernalia.

Officers and inmates agree that it is the 20 percent who will not abide by the rules that make it tough on the other 80 percent. "Most of them," says one officer, "go about their business and do their time. But you have to remember why they are in here. They are here because they couldn't follow the rules.

And nearly every one of these guys has the potential and the ability to explode at any time."

Adds an inmate, "You got all kinds of mentalities in here."

It is not the threat of physical violence that maintains order in the prison but the threat of losing one's privileges. While many of the officers voiced concerns that the inmates have it soft, the same officers also maintained that things like recreation, visitors, and special events are the only freedoms the inmates have left, and they don't want to lose them.

Order is also maintained, in a sense, by the inmates themselves. "You'd be surprised," says one officer, "at how many of these guys are anti-drugs. They don't want to be around those who use drugs and they don't want the officers shaking down the cells because they're afraid that something they aren't supposed to have themselves will be uncovered.

"Also, a lot of these guys—especially the older ones—want to be left alone and treated with a certain amount of respect. If someone on their block is causing problems, they know that isn't going to happen."

Among the 215 officers assigned to Lebanon are 29 women. Views on female officers in a men's prison vary among the male officers. Some feel they have a calming effect, while others feel they are not capable of performing all of the jobs a correctional officer must do.

CONTRABAND: Inmates improvise to make weapons and tools. LEFT TO RIGHT: a knife made with a piece of metal from a computer; a homemade tattoo gun hooked to a nine volt battery; a stinger, which can be plugged into a wall socket to heat coffee; and a knife made from plexiglass.

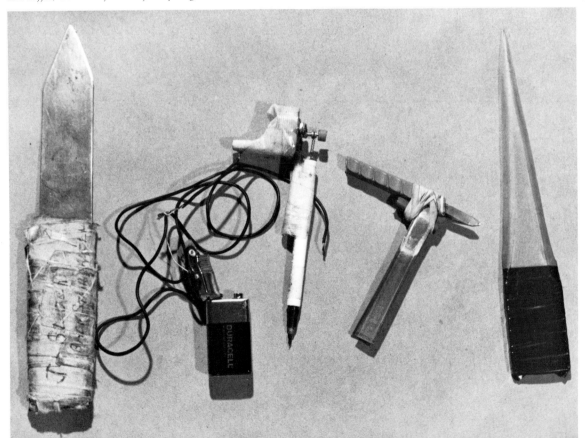

15

MAIL ROOM: All incoming mail is inspected by an officer to ensure that no contraband, such as drugs or weapons, is smuggled into the prison. Legal materials are opened in the presence of the inmate.

Opposite Page—*AFTERNOON SHIFT: A senior female officer at Lebanon.*

"The only job I'm not allowed to have," says one female officer, "is a cell-block assignment. I'm not allowed in where the men actually live. Other than that, I do every job in the institution."

Another female officer says that initially, some of the inmates peppered her with verbal abuse about being hard up for a man, but as soon as they saw that she was going to conduct herself the same as the male officers, it stopped.

"Some of the guys, especially the weaker ones," says another female officer, "will sometimes push the rules to the limit or intentionally do things you'll get down on them for because they are so starved for attention. But for the most part, I don't have any problems."

The inmates themselves have varied opinions about the opposite sex working at the prison. Says one inmate derisively, "A woman can't discipline a man. You got somebody doing a life bit, and this woman here telling him to shut up? Uh-uh. There's one here, she's creating a lot of s - - - ."

The same inmate, however, admits that, "If she tries it on me, I'll just suck it in. Because I want to go home."

Other inmates maintain that they don't care one way or the other about what sex an officer is in terms of performing duties, but that having women around creates sexual tension. As one man put it, "I ain't got nothing against women's lib or none of that. Equal opportunity. But you got guys in here doing life bits [sentences]. They ain't been close to a woman. And here all of a sudden, there are women in the penitentiary. Walking around with tight pants on, you know. S - - - jiggling around. I mean, what the hell, you know. I got one where I work. And I ain't had no p - - - in ten years. You can imagine how I feel. I don't think that's right."

Opposite Page—PATROL CAR: Officers patrol outside the prison perimeter 24 hours a day. The patrol officers and the officers in the towers are the only ones who carry guns.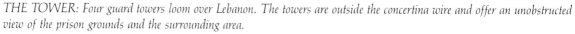

THE TOWER: Four guard towers loom over Lebanon. The towers are outside the concertina wire and offer an unobstructed view of the prison grounds and the surrounding area.

HALL DUTY: Female officers are not allowed to work on the cell blocks, but they perform all of the other duties the male officers do.

Opposite Page—*CONCERTINA WIRE: A double row of concertina wire surrounds the institution. The area between the wire is equipped with a sensitive alarm system. Although the wire is razor-sharp, inmates sometimes do attempt to climb over it.*

$\longrightarrow$

3

Crimes and Misdemeanors

The inmate is dressed in the white uniform assigned to those who work in the dining hall. His hands are cuffed to a belt around his waist. He stares up at the elevated desk and the three officers on the Rules Infraction Board. The charges against the inmate haven't been read yet, but the look on his face says that he expects to be found guilty and that he expects to be punished.

The senior officer peers down at the inmate over the top of his glasses. In an emotionless monotone that indicates he's been conducting similar hearings for a long time and that nothing surprises him anymore, he reads the charges: the inmate is accused of stealing four uncooked chicken breasts from the kitchen.

The inmate, who appears to be in his early twenties, admits that he stole the chicken, but defends his actions by explaining that he was going to take it to the bakery, cook it, and share it with other inmates. He also argues that other officers had allowed this practice at the end of a shift.

When he finishes his plea, the inmate is told to go into the adjoining room. He shuffles out, convinced that the three officers weren't listening.

It's easy to see why he would feel that way. The entire proceeding lasted no more than a couple of minutes. Throughout the hearing, one officer was continually shuffling papers, while another was busy writing something on a state-issued form. All three appeared to be doing two or three tasks at once.

But the officers were paying attention. Not only did they listen to what the young inmate had to say, they had read the written report earlier in its entirety. They also know the prison well enough to know that when the inmate stated that other officers had allowed him to take some chicken at the end of his shift, he was probably telling the truth.

The officers spend about 10 seconds reaching a verdict and another 30 seconds deciding on the proper punishment. The inmate is called back in, and

THE RULES INFRACTION BOARD: Inmates who commit serious infractions while at Lebanon go before an internal court called the Rules Infraction Board (RIB). If the inmate is found guilty, the board members may impose a sentence of up to 15 days in isolation.

the senior officer announces their decision: they find the inmate guilty, but suspend his sentence.

The inmate stares up at them in disbelief, knowing that they could have sent him to disciplinary control, or "the hole" as it is commonly called. The hole is an isolation cell to which inmates may be sentenced to a maximum of 15 days. While confined to the hole, inmates are not allowed to go to recreation, the dayroom, the library, or any other recreational or social activity. Restrictions are also placed on showers, commissary, and visiting privileges.

The officers pull the file on the next case. It's a typical day for the Rules Infraction Board. So far, they've found two inmates guilty of using drugs, one inmate was convicted of assaulting his cellmate because he wouldn't stop singing, and one inmate was found not guilty of throwing a shampoo bottle at an officer.

PLEADING THE CASE: Inmates in local control are issued jumpsuits. Because there is no air conditioning, they are allowed to peel their jumpsuits to their waists.

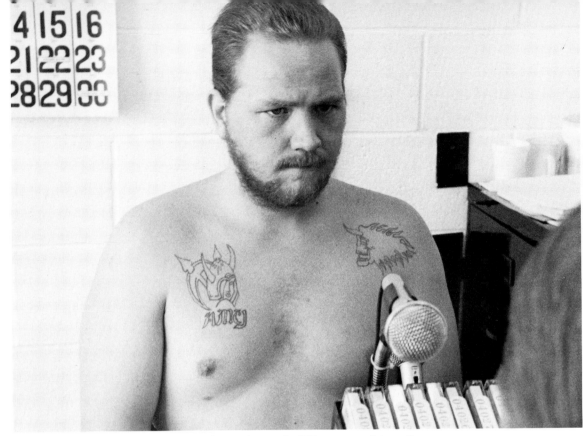

DAY IN COURT: An inmate listens as the members of the RIB announce their verdict.

Among the inmates, the general feeling is that you cannot get a fair deal from the Rules Infraction Board. "They can do anything they want," says one inmate. "You don't have to do nothin', but if they want to get you, they can."

Adds another, "If they think you've been up to something, they'll write you up for no reason, then find you guilty just to teach you a lesson."

The Rules Infraction Board is an internal courtroom. Inmates appear before the board when they have committed a serious offense or when they wish to appeal a guilty verdict handed down by a hearing officer on a lesser charge.

The rules governing the behavior of Lebanon inmates sometimes appear to be petty ones. Shirts must be tucked in. A beard may be no longer than one inch from the face. Hair cannot extend over the ear or over the shirt collar. When in the hallways, inmates must walk along the right-hand wall.

Each of these rules, however, has a logical reason behind it. As one senior officer points out, "It's amazing what you can hide in your hair or your beard if they're long enough. A knife, dope. It's pretty easy to do. And that's why we enforce the haircut regulations so earnestly. It cuts down on contraband and weapons."

Requiring shirts to be tucked also decreases the possibility of an inmate concealing a weapon, and the rule about always walking along the right-hand wall allows the officers an unobstructed view from one end of a corridor to the other.

"If we let them clog up the middle," says one officer, "it's hard to spot a fight or some sort of deal going down."

The disposition of these types of infractions are, however, usually handled at the time of the violation. Sometimes it's a matter of simply telling the inmate to correct the infraction, or giving the offender a verbal reprimand.

"I only write my conduct reports for extreme cases," says one officer. "I'll make them stand at the main wall by the captain's office, but I'm not a big ticket writer. I try and get my point across by doing my own job, not by throwing it on the captain or throwing it on the Rules Infraction Board when they have cases stacked to here."

The officer says that some of the inmates will push as far as they can to see what they can get away with, then back off as soon as the officer shows that he or she means business.

The shift captain agrees. "They'll try anything," he says. "For example, if their shirt isn't tucked in, they'll watch you to see if you're looking at them, or they'll get so close to you before they'll tuck it in. They'll take it to the wire. They know the rules as good or better than we do. And they know how to deal with each officer."

But not every infraction can be handled by a scolding or having someone stand against the wall. Inside the prison, like outside, some of the violations are very serious, such as the case the Rules Infraction Board must now deal with. An inmate has been accused of dealing drugs. He pleads innocent and maintains he has been off drugs since he came to Lebanon. But the officers know better. The inmate was before the board several months earlier, too strung out on drugs to defend himself.

The officers quickly agree that the inmate is guilty and they also agree that his sentence will be transfer to a maximum security prison.

Although the arresting officer in this case reported that the inmate had initially admitted his crime, the inmate now says that he did not.

"He doesn't want to be known as a snitch," explains one of the officers after the inmate leaves the room. "That's why he now wants to have it on record that he didn't sign the statement. He's afraid they're going to label him as a snitch."

A snitch is a label none of the inmates want to wear, but both inmates and officers admit that it is a common practice.

"This is a snitch's prison," says an inmate who is serving a life sentence. "Down at Lucasville [Southern Ohio Correctional Facility], you know, you mind your own business, you do your own time. But here, you got guys running around and telling on each other. It's tough to do your time in someplace like this."

Page 26—LOCAL CONTROL: Inmates are placed in local control while they wait for their case to be heard by the RIB. The board may also recommend local control instead of isolation when an inmate is found guilty of breaking one of the prison's rules. Local control allows more privileges than isolation but fewer than in a regular cell block.

Page 27—MAXIMUM SECURITY: The maximum security block at Lebanon has wire cages surrounding the cell doors. The block is the only one where the cells have no windows to the outside.

Although the inmate admits that Lebanon is a safer environment than some of the other prisons he's been in, he also wants to be left alone to serve his time and has difficulty with what he sees as petty snitching and enforcement.

"If you want to smoke a joint," adds another inmate, "and you step out on the range, chances are before the night's over the police are going to be up there shaking you down, tearing your house up, ripping your s - - - open."

An officer who has worked at Lebanon for 10 years agrees. But he has an understandably different opinion on the value of snitching. "It stops a lot of things. It prevents drug deals from going down. It prevents escapes. And it prevents people from getting hurt. You have to remember that we not only have to keep order in here, but we have to keep the inmates safe."

Most of the officers feel that the snitching is no greater at Lebanon than it is at other institutions. Says one officer, "Most of these guys are snitches in one form or another. Most of them are in here because someone told on them. They carry that trait into the prison.

"Personally, I don't think there's any more snitching here than anywhere else. I think it's simply that we enforce the rules more than some other prisons might."

ISOLATION CELL: While in isolation, inmates are not allowed to take part in activities, and visiting privileges are restricted.

THE HOLE: The view from inside an isolation cell, referred to by inmates as "the hole."

EXERCISE CAGE, MAXIMUM SECURITY: Because exercise is prescribed by law, even maximum security inmates are entitled to one hour of recreation three times a week. They are allowed to exercise only in the cage provided.

Life in the Joint

"Henry" is 50 years old and has been in prison four different times. He's spent over 23 years in various institutions, and he thinks he sees a difference in the type of inmate now incarcerated at Lebanon.

"When I was bit'n [serving time] in the late 1960s, early 1970s, people's values was more important to them than drugs was. People got strung out on drugs, sure enough, but we had some guidelines, man. Some moral values that we stood by. Today, people don't have no moral values. Kids today are not raised like we was raised.

"I'm not proud to say I got four numbers. I'm not proud to say I've got over 23 years in at these camps. But I have never experienced nothing like I'm experiencing now."

Another inmate agrees. "Probably 90 percent of those who come in here are for drug-related crimes," he says. "The sheet might not say nothin' about drugs. It might be burglary or armed robbery. But it was drugs that got them there. And that's one of the differences with these younger guys."

Many of the older inmates—those over 40—also feel that it's the young ones who create most of the problems inside the prison. Says one, "The guards ain't going to have the problems out of guys like me that they're going to have out of the younger guys. We want to go through this without a whole lot of hassle."

It's a statement that many officers tend to agree with. "The older guys," says one veteran officer, "have been through this before, or are serving longer sentences. They know how to get along. I worked here when it was a reformatory. I don't have nearly the problems now that it's a close security prison. But one thing with the older ones—when you do have a problem, you have a real problem."

While some of the officers feel that things haven't really changed very much in prison, most agree that the older inmates are different. "They've mellowed out," is the way several put it. Adds one officer, "It's just like you and me. We were a lot wilder, a lot more reckless when we were in our twenties. But you get older, you accept more responsibility, you get a little smarter."

While one might expect a pecking order among the inmates based on the types of crimes they committed, that does not seem to be the rule. The inmates appear to be more concerned with what a person does inside than what he did on the outside, with two notable exceptions: child molesters and rapists are considered the bottom of the barrel.

CELL 22: Inmates refer to their cell as their house. Each inmate must have his picture identification card displayed. The top picture identifies the inmate in the upper bunk, and the bottom picture identifies the inmate in the lower bunk.

INMATE IN CELL BLOCK A: *Even with work assignments and recreation privileges, most of an inmate's time is spent in his cell.*

"Child molesters are going to have a tough time of it," says one inmate. "They'll [the other inmates] make it difficult for them every chance they get. For the most part, nobody seems to care what kind of crime you did, but nobody likes child molesters and tree jumpers [rapists]."

Several of the inmates and several of the officers state that while most of the time you don't know what another inmate is in for unless he tells you, the word on child molesters and rapists somehow gets around quickly.

"You have to remember," adds one of the officers, "many of these guys have families. And they don't take kindly to the thought of someone messing with their children."

More important than the crime committed is the way in which an inmate handles himself once he's inside. Inmates and officers alike seem to divide the population into two categories: strong and weak. And in prison, nobody has much sympathy for the weak.

"The feeling in here," says one inmate, "is that whatever you get, you deserve it. The weak deserve it. They had a choice, and they are paying the consequences. They're not playing the game right. That's the way of the prison. Survival of the fittest."

Physical strength is respected at Lebanon, and many of the inmates admit

ELDER STATESMAN: *Lebanon's oldest inmate is 78 years old.*

that their main reason for lifting weights is to become—or at least look—strong.

"The physical part is important," says one, "because people can see that. I weighed 135, 140 pounds when I came in here. I'm up to about 190 now. It helps."

From inmates and officers alike comes the same advice for new arrivals: Don't gamble. Stay away from the homosexuals. And don't show weakness.

One inmate prefers a direct approach. "It depends on the situation," he says. "If they're going to try to make a punk [homosexual] out of you, the best thing is to just shank [knife] 'em. You're going to go to the hole for six months, but you're going to get your respect."

There are, of course, less drastic paths the inmates can follow. Many inmates find that they have to actually fight someone only once in order to

A SINGLE CELL: Because of crowded conditions, usually only honor or merit status inmates have single cells. Two pin-ups are allowed, and a maximum of six items may be taped to the walls. Cell lights and windows must remain uncovered.

prove their point, and winning doesn't seem to be as important as simply stand-ing up for oneself. As one inmate put it, "The consequences of backing down are more severe than taking a beating."

Others admit to bluffing their way through by acting tough, while others practice an aura of being "hard" or crazy.

Even those who are not physically strong can survive, if they know how to carry themselves.

"You've got to have an attitude," says one inmate. "A real assertive attitude. The attitude that you're gonna get what's coming to you no matter who stands in your way."

Adds another inmate, "You have to be mentally strong. You have to keep on going and not collapse under all the pressure. There is a certain amount of physical strength you must have, but mental strength is number one."

Says one officer, "If somebody comes up to you and says, 'Gimme your pack of cigarettes,' and you give in to him, you're weak. Now that guy knows that tomorrow he knows where to come and get the next pack.

"You got to be able to stand your ground. And just by standing your ground, you'll show other people that you're nobody to play with."

Adds another officer, "I got one new guy came in last week. Didn't know which way to turn, who to turn to for help. He came in and told me, 'I'm scared to death, man. I don't know what to do. I try to be friends with people, and they're rubbing me the wrong way. They want sex from me and I've only been here two days. A guy is trying to take my commissary from me. What do I do?'

"So I go up and I get two of what I feel are the good guys. The ones that have some authority in the block. The ones that can make other people under-stand. And I set him down with the good guys and I say, 'Hey, look over him. Show him who to associate with and who to stay away from. Tell him how to play the game.'"

Those who do not learn to play the game properly can often find them-selves an easy target for the homosexuals. As one inmate bluntly put it, "In here, if you don't be the man you're supposed to be, you'll be the woman you don't want to be."

THE SHOWER ROOM: Each range in a cell block has one shower room. No more than three inmates are allowed in the shower at one time.

Being "turned out" (forced into becoming a homosexual) represents the ultimate degradation in prison, and, consequently, the ultimate form of weakness.

One inmate puts it this way: "Little guys come in here. They never done no time before, and they keep getting into these vices [gambling, drugs, etc.]. So they owe this guy and they owe that guy. So they have to do sexual favors. A lot of them get turned out that way. A lot of them are chosen as soon as they get off the bus."

Although extortion seems to be the primary vehicle for "turning someone out," there is also the direct approach. "A lot of times, it's just a matter of a strong guy picking on a weak guy," says one officer. The same officer feels that about half of Lebanon's homosexuals were gay before they entered prison.

Many of the inmates differentiate between "pitchers" and "catchers." That is, the person who plays the male role—the pitcher—is not considered a homosexual, but the catcher—the female role—is considered a "fag" or "bitch."

"Yeah, they make that distinction," smiles one officer. "I never figured it out. Whether you're a pitcher or a catcher, you're still playing on the same ball team."

An inmate agrees. "I hear these guys saying, 'Man, I gotta get me a bitch.' And some of them will actually break down and cry when they get into a fight with their bitch, like they was going through a divorce or something. Man, I don't understand that. It ain't natural for a man to love another man that way."

Although homosexuality is not condoned by Lebanon's administration, the officers admit that it is nearly impossible to control. One officer describes it this way:

"Inmates know the habits of the officers. They know what they do. They know that at six o'clock when the chow cart comes by, he's going to sit down for at least 20 minutes and eat his meal. And while he's sitting at his desk, a guy opens up his door, lays down on his belly, sneaks down the third range like a snake, goes in another cell, commits the act, and comes back.

"In the shop area: Two inmates go over to the supervisor and start asking him questions and bull - - - with him, distracting him, while two others go over here to a secluded area and commit their act. There are a thousand possible ways."

The officials at Lebanon do not permit inmates to use facial makeup or wear brassieres or bikini panties or otherwise dress like women, but a shift captain says the officers occasionally find women's clothing. "They get it smuggled in somehow. And when we find it, we confiscate it."

Some inmates, however, can be very creative. Kool Aid is used for eye shadow, lipstick, and blush.

"Some of these guys," says one inmate, "will wear tight pants, go work out and do squats and stuff so they build up their a - -. Try to get it big and look like a woman's a - -."

CELL MATES: *Cells at Lebanon are six feet by eight feet, and most house two men. The older inmate (in terms of time served at Lebanon) is allowed to have his television out. The newer inmate must store his beneath the bunk.*

INMATE WITH HOT WATER BOTTLE: *This inmate has circulatory difficulty and is allowed to have a hot water bottle to help keep him warm.*

LIFE IN THE BLOCK: These inmates and officer take a break to pose for the camera.

While both inmates and officers agree that rapes do take place, they also agree that it is far less common than the mass media would have us believe.

"If you just watch who you hang with and don't get into the vices, you can pretty much keep to yourself and not get hassled," is the common refrain among the inmates

Keeping to yourself in prison is nearly impossible, however. Because of the crowded conditions, single cell occupancy is pretty much limited to those on honor or merit status. For most, they are always being watched by other inmates and/or officers.

"You're constantly on stage here," says one inmate. "There are no secrets in here. Whatever you do, it's going to be all over."

Adds another inmate, "There is absolutely no privacy in here. The only time you can be yourself is right before you go to sleep and your cellie is above you or below you and can't see you. S - - -, you can't even go to the toilet without your cellie watching you."

This "togetherness" also magnifies the significance of even the most minor confrontation between two inmates. As one man put it, "Out on the streets, if you don't get along with someone, you can walk away from him. But in here, if you don't get along with somebody, you're still around him. It's just part of life in prison."

Although the inmates at Lebanon have associates—people they hang around with—very few admit to having friends. "You can converse with somebody," says one inmate, "but you can't be a friend. You get too close to some-body and the first thing they think is that you're weak or a homosexual."

The typical feeling among the inmates is that they live in a dog-eat-dog environment and that they must be continually on guard in order to protect themselves, their possessions, and their manhood. Despite being surrounded by 2,000 inmates, they feel isolated. And they tend not to trust each other.

"Trust them? Hell no! In my experience I've been screwed over by guys and I've seen a lot of other guys get screwed over.

"You might move into a new block and the guy in the next cell starts talk-ing to you. You begin to buddy up and then he asks for some smokes. You figure that he'll pay you back or give you some if you need 'em. But later on you ask him if you can get some, and he comes off like 'F - - - you.' He may even try to get more off you, take whatever else you got. You think he's a friend, but you find out the hard way that there are no friends in here. I can count the friends I've had in here on one finger."

Adds another inmate, "Every one of your friends could do you in. You don't know them any better than they know you. You never really know who they are."

Many of the inmates describe their actions inside the prison as a front. One man maintains that he is really an emotional person, but that he cannot show any emotion at Lebanon.

"It's all a front. How I look, how I carry myself, and how I talk."

Inmates especially confide that emotions other than anger and contempt are considered unmasculine and must be avoided at all cost.

One inmate, who has not been incarcerated for very long, admitted that he sometimes has a tough time of it after visiting with relatives. But he adds that when he goes back to the block, he tells no one about his feelings for fear that they will think he is weak.

THE DINING HALL: *The quality of the food is extremely important to the inmates. Officers say that if a bad meal is served, the inmates will complain for hours.*

Adds another, "You can't be sensitive in here. That or being kind is a sign of weakness. When you see someone who is emotional or kind, he is a mark. He'll be used up sexually or money-wise."

Spending too much time with the officers is also frowned on by most inmates. Although many say that the officers treat them well and that they don't have anything against them, they also feel that it's best to keep your distance or else you will develop a reputation as a snitch.

The officers, too, try to keep their distance. "There are a few guys in here I feel sorry for," says one, adding that in some instances he can understand what they did and doesn't always agree with the sentence they received.

"But I can't afford to show favoritism. I have to treat them all equally."

Says another officer, "There are a couple of guys who work for me that appear to be squared away. But you can't get close to them. It's better to treat them with respect than closeness."

Constant activity is the ingredient most men cite as the key to doing time. Such comments as, "You can't let your mind go back to the streets; you got to concentrate on what's here and just take it a day at a time," are common among the inmates. Common also is the sentiment that you go to work, exercise, get involved in some programs, and keep busy.

GUITAR PLAYERS: Recreation time in the "yard" is extremely valuable to the inmates, not only for physical activity but for a chance to relax and interact with others.

Page 43—THE WEIGHT LIFTER: This man is the champion weight lifter at Lebanon. He can dead lift 700 pounds and bench press 380 pounds.

PUMPING IRON: Weight lifting is by far the most popular activity among the inmates. Most inmates say that in addition to the exercise, it is important in prison to look physically strong.

Many of the inmates have televisions or radios in their cells. The prison operates both a regular and a law library. While books in the law library may not be checked out, books and periodicals can be checked out of the regular library for two-week periods. Inmates are allowed to have up to five books in their cells, along with four magazines and two newspapers. College students are allowed to have an additional 15 books.

One inmate says that, for the most part, it's easy to pass the time. He did fabricating and construction work on the outside and has a similar job inside, which he enjoys. At $78 a month he is one of the higher paid inmates and he can easily afford to purchase extras from the commissary. He works out a lot and he enjoys reading.

"For 11 months out of the year, it's easy. But from November to December, it takes me a whole year to get through it. You can't turn on the television without hearing "Jingle Bells" and "Merry Christmas" and all that s - - -! On Christmas Eve, I cried. The loneliness hit me so hard. I realized what I was missing by being in here."

Holidays appear to be tough on most of the inmates. The officers describe holiday time as very subdued. The inmates keep to themselves. Ironically, holidays also tend to offer up fewer rule infractions.

"I think it's because there is less interaction," says one officer. "The inmates really keep to themselves during those periods."

Life at Lebanon is always by the numbers, and the prison infirmary is no exception. Sick call is held twice daily for routine treatment, and emergency cases are handled as needed. The infirmary is a full-service clinic complete with an x-ray machine, dental equipment, an eye examination room, a doctor's office, and 10 beds.

Inmates who take controlled narcotics, who are suspected of being unreliable, or who abuse their medication must go to the infirmary to get their pills. Some inmates are self-medicated, and some are allowed small quantities of such things as Tylenol, Mylanta, and athlete's foot cream.

INMATE AT IRONING BOARD: Each cell block has an area where inmates may do their personal laundry and ironing, always under the close supervision of an officer.

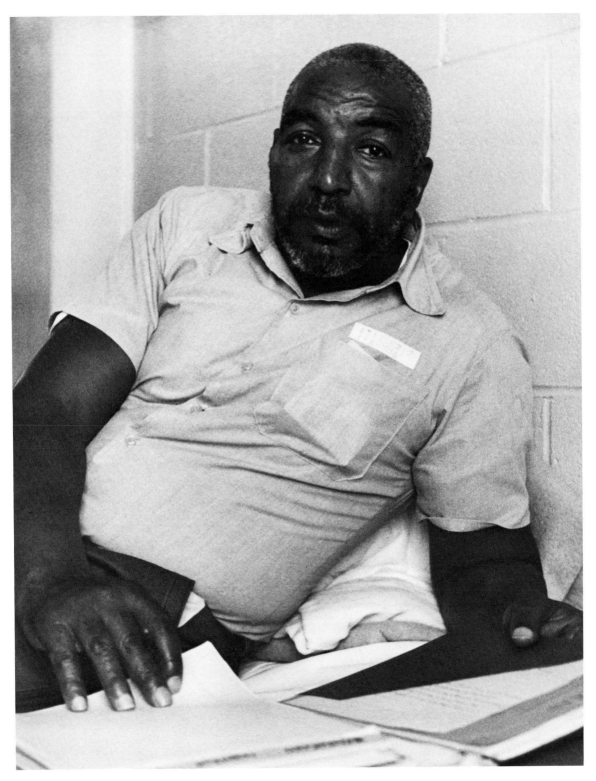

INMATE READING: *The prison library supplies inmates with fiction and nonfiction material.*

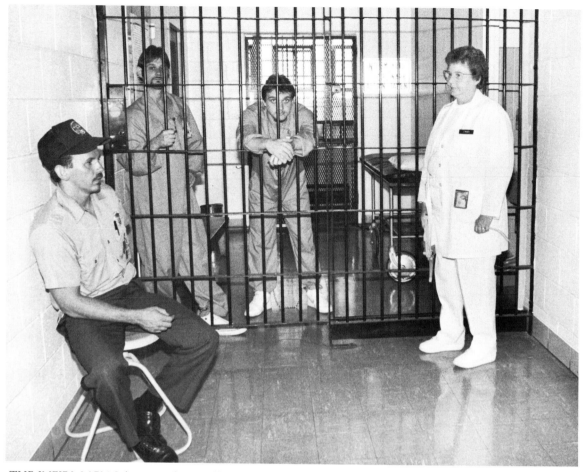

THE INFIRMARY: Lebanon employs a full-time nurse and a full-time doctor to treat routine medical problems.

Opposite Page—*THE DISPENSARY: Inmates who are on medication must go to the dispensary to receive their pills. In some instances, inmates are allowed to self-medicate.* ⟶

The typical day at Lebanon begins at 6:30 a.m.; breakfast is served 15 minutes later. Inmates must report to their job assignments no later than 8 a.m. Lunch is served between 10:30 a.m. and 12 noon, and dinner begins at 4:30 p.m.

Deviations from the schedule are seldom appreciated by the inmates, especially when it comes to meal time. "If central control makes a mistake and calls the wrong block, you'll immediately start hearing the complaints," says a senior captain. "Food is very important to them. If you look at history, you'll find that most riots have started in the mess hall."

The inmates learn to adapt to the rigid schedule, and they learn to look forward to the small pleasures of recreation, visits, and meals. For those serving long sentences, comfort is a relevant term. Says one inmate, "I got my own cell, I work third shift. I get recreation passes every day. Now, that's a lot. That's a lot for me to have, being locked up. And with the bit that I'm doing, it just ain't going to get no better than this."

5

The Importance of Recreation

By the time he reached his mid-twenties, "David" was a testimonial to the American dream. Reared in a middle-class family, he had attended college for a few years, then went on to radio and television production. At various times, he also worked in advertising and public relations, and once did promotional work for a nationally known boxer.

Today, David is serving a nine-year sentence for bank robbery, and his boxing promotions are limited to setting up matches inside Lebanon.

David is the inmates' boxing commissioner and a member of the African Cultural Organization. The latter group sponsors matches—sometimes against opponents from the outside—and raises money for the United Negro College Fund. Their most recent effort netted $450.

David feels recreational activities, such as the boxing matches, are "tremendously important" to the inmates. "All these anxieties build up in here. You need some sort of pleasurable outlet that is, at the same time, wholesome. I think the recreation helps keep guys who are in an abnormal environment normalized.

"After a big event like the boxing match," he adds, "you can see a calming effect. It seems to help the guys burn off that excess energy."

A senior captain who served as one of the scorekeepers for the boxing match agrees. "Recreation is real important. If we kept them locked up 24 hours a day, we'd have a lot more problems. In fact, you have a lot more rule infractions in the winter months, when it's harder to get outside and the recreation is limited."

He says security is tighter when the institution has large numbers at these events, but that they seem to go on relatively incident-free. "They know that if they mess up, they're going to lose their privileges."

FUNDRAISER: *This boxing match was sponsored by the African Cultural Organization and raised $450 for the United Negro College Fund.*

The captain says the inmates look forward to the boxing matches and softball tournaments and other recreational activities and that it helps keep their minds off their situation.

"It's just like on the outside," he adds. "If you have a bowling tournament coming up next week, that's about the only thing you're going to think of for about a week, even though you're working and everything else. Same thing with these guys."

The 49-year-old David enjoys working with the boxers. "I try to work with them and create a positive environment. It gives me a sense of self-worth. It's a way of atoning for what I did.

"I look back on it now and I think I wanted to get caught. At one point in my life I was making six to eight hundred dollars a week. But I was destroying myself with the madness of drugs. I got heavily into debt, and I went looking for an easy way out. I don't feel good about that. But maybe I can work with these kids and convince them that there's another way to live your life."

DO NOT HANG ON RIM

HITTING THE COURTS: Inmates may attend recreation in the yard whenever they are off work.

David says that he personally has watched a number of inmates give up on drugs and other penitentiary hustles after they became heavily involved in recreational activities. "I think for the first couple of years a lot of guys in here thought I was running some sort of con, but now the word is out that we're on the up and up and trying to find alternatives to the madness that got us in here in the first place."

Like most inmates, David works out himself, usually on a daily basis. "I ran track in high school, so that's what I do here to keep in shape. I lift a little weights to tone up, but for the most part, it's running."

For another inmate named Mathew the main form of recreation is weight-lifting, and his well-sculpted body leaves no reason to doubt his claims that he can dead lift 700 pounds and bench press nearly 400 pounds.

Mathew has been lifting weights seriously for about three years. He started primarily because the prison's small gymnasium made it difficult to get on the basketball court. Now, he is a champion lifter at Lebanon.

"It helps get me through my time," he says. "I try to find something positive to do with my time. I did commit the crime, and I know I gotta pay the price for what I done. I accepted that early on."

Mathew, like David, also enjoys helping younger inmates, but only, he says, if they are serious. "If they're just off on some ego trip, I don't want any part of them. I'm serious about body-building. I'm 42 years old. But I go out and play basketball and the other guys will be out of wind and I'll still be running up and down the court."

Mathew's weightlifting abilities are, he says, something the other inmates respect, sometimes to his detriment. Before a recent meet, Mathew says someone planted contraband in his work area so that he would be confined to his cell for the weekend and not be able to compete.

Although weightlifting appears to be the most common form of recreation among the inmates and many admit that physical strength inside the prison is important, there are other forms of recreation, such as softball, basketball, horseshoes, and even a miniature golf course.

Not all recreation at Lebanon is physical, of course. On any given day, dozens of inmates simply sunbathe while listening to their radios. Others play guitars, while some simply walk around the track, enjoying their free time.

Inmate organizations and prison officials also offer other forms of entertainment, such as movies, talent contests, and so on. There is usually some sort of special activity about once a week. Recreation is mandated by state law, and inmates are allowed to use the prison facilities whenever they are not working. Inmates in isolation are permitted one-hour sessions three times a week, and their recreation is confined to a small cage.

THE MAIN EVENT: Boxing matches are held several times a year. The referees are inmates and the announcer was brought in from outside.

6

Different Strokes for Different Folks

There are 10 cellblocks and three isolation units at Lebanon. Each of the cellblocks has an ice machine. The machines were purchased by the Miami Valley Jaycees, an inmate organization affiliated with the Ohio and International Jaycees.

The Jaycees have a membership fee, and they raise additional funds by sponsoring special events, selling cassette tapes, and operating the photographer's stand in the visiting room.

Other prison groups include the African Cultural Organization; the Gavel Club; and the Seventh Step Organization, a self-awareness group. At various times, these organizations have assisted the homeless on the outside, provided scholarship money for college students, and purchased equipment for the other inmates.

Inmates at Lebanon may further their education through GED (General Education Development), high school, vocational, and college classes. The psychological services department of the prison offers both group and individualized counseling, and various church-sponsored groups are brought in on a weekly basis. These services, argues one officer, are extremely important when it comes to helping inmates pass the time. "If I were counseling a new inmate, I'd tell him to get involved. It's going to make it go a whole lot easier. When you finish with one program, go on to another. When you finish that, go on to something else."

The programs can, of course, do more for the inmate than simply help him pass the time. A study by Wilmington College, which operates both associate and bachelor's degree programs at Lebanon, shows that paroled inmates who completed the college program had a recidivism rate of only 11 percent, while the national recidivism rate runs close to 70 percent.

COLLEGE CAMPUS: Wilmington College offers associate and bachelor's degree programs for inmates. Inmates must be within four years of their parole date and must meet strict criteria while enrolled. For example, an inmate who misses two classes in a semester is dismissed not only from class but from the entire program.

Says a 50-year-old inmate who is serving his fourth sentence, "The best advice I can give to a new guy coming in the joint is to get in the college program. They're going to need that when they get out."

Groups like Seventh Step and Alcoholics Anonymous can also increase an inmate's sense of self-worth and assist him with the problems that partially caused his incarceration in the first place.

Clark, an inmate who has served nine years in prison, feels these organizations are invaluable. "You can get anything you want in here. Drugs, gambling, anything. I want to stay away from that. That's why I'm finishing my college education. That's why I'm involved in Jaycees and the African Cultural Organization. You have to arrive at some spiritual realization. You have to want to turn your life around and these programs help."

For another inmate, the prison chapel has been a big influence. After serving a five-year sentence in Lucasville, he was on the streets only 10 days before he was busted for receiving stolen property. He is currently serving an 18-month sentence, and he seems determined to turn things around.

"I don't want to be a loser," he says. "I keep a low profile. I go to work, I exercise, and I write letters. I've had some personal problems come up on the outside, and the chaplain has been a big help in getting me through all of this. And I plan to enroll in the college program next semester."

Different Strokes for Different Folks

But not every inmate sees the value in the prison's services. "I think the college program is sincere," says one inmate, "but the rest is bull - - -. I went to the church about three times," he adds. "and that's when I realized it was nothing but a place for the gumpys [homosexuals] to meet. I haven't been back.

"I come in here, you know, I figured I'd do my time and I'd leave. I didn't have none of that on my mind. When I went to the parole board that's the first f - - - thing they said. You know what they asked me? They said, 'If you went on a trip, wouldn't you pack a suitcase?'

"I said, 'Yeah.' And they said, 'So what did you pack for the parole board?'

"And that's why they give me four more years."

The inmate, who is serving 15 to life for a murder charge, feels that as long as he stays out of isolation and keeps his nose clean, the prison shouldn't ask anything more of him. But, as much as he dislikes the thought, he admits that he will—as he gets closer to his next parole date—join some of the organizations.

"You got to have them programs if you want to make parole," he says. "If you don't do it for yourself, you do it for the parole board."

THE CHAPEL: In addition to religious services, the chapel hosts numerous meetings and speakers from the outside.

Adds another inmate, "If you want to take them seriously and you want to go to them and apply yourself, I'm sure they can probably help, or at least point you in the right direction.

"For me, I'm not too keen on sitting and doing things. I like to be active. I know myself better than anybody, and I know that sitting in some place and listening to somebody talking isn't going to do it for me.

"The same people who go through all these programs are back in here for two or three numbers. So I don't see what it did for them. I've talked to guys who have been locked up three or four times, and they say, 'Yeah, I went through all that. I used to be the leader of it.'"

THE CLASSROOM: The prison maintains an educational area with classrooms for college programs. Students who attend college are considered to be at work while they take classes.

INMATE AND MOTHER AT GRADUATION: Inmates who graduate from Wilmington College's program participate in a formal commencement ceremony with relatives in attendance.

VISITORS
REGISTER

ORS MUST HAVE
O I.D. NO SOCIAL
RITY CARDS OR
CERTIFICATES
PTED. YOU MUST
INMATE'S NUMBER.
SITOR REGISTERED
R P.M. NO PACK
R P.M. NO PACK
KENDS OR HOLIDAYS!

7

They Also Serve Who Come to Visit

The visiting room at Lebanon is an emotional place. An elderly woman visits with her grandson. A young woman brings her infant son to visit his father. Another inmate sits with his wife and two children. Outside on the picnic bench a couple embraces. A few are engaged in rather animated discussions, while others are subdued, apparently content just to sit and look at each other for a few minutes.

The visitors are not allowed to bring in food or beverages, but there are a variety of vending machines, and the tables are filled with soft drink containers and snacks. The inmates themselves are not allowed to handle money, so their guests must make the actual purchases.

The visiting room, which seats about 200 people, is about half full. The picnic area outside, which holds another 150 or so people, is also at less than capacity, allowing most of the inmates a semblance of privacy with their visitors.

Visiting hours are held daily, except for holidays. The typical inmate is allowed two visits per month from each person on his approved visiting list. Visitors are limited to immediate family members and two friends.

The visits are for three-hour periods, but as one inmate puts it, "By the time they call you down and everything, it's usually not much more than a couple of hours."

Family members who travel more than 150 miles to the prison may double up. That is, they may stay twice as long, but the time counts as two visits. Inmates on honor or merit status are given increased privileges, as are those who are within 30 days of being released.

For many inmates, weekly or monthly visits from their loved ones are what gets them through their time. "I don't know what I'd do if my folks didn't come every week," says one inmate. "I live for those visits."

VISITOR REGISTRATION: All visitors must be on an approved list before their visit. When entering the institution, visitors must register and receive a pass.

"That's one privilege most of them don't want to lose," says an officer who has spent many hours assigned to the visiting room. "Visiting, food, and recreation. Those are the three most important elements to these guys."

"It's hard to watch, sometimes," says a veteran officer. "I don't feel sorry for the guy doing time. He's in here for a reason. But I feel sorry for the parents sometimes. They didn't do anything, but now they have to suffer through it."

The officer quickly adds, however, that for the most part, he's become immune to it because of the scams he's seen visitors try to pull over the years.

"Most contraband in here comes in from the outside," he says. "And they come in through that visiting room."

Other officers agree. "We arrest two or three visitors a month for trying to smuggle drugs in here," says one. "We had to arrest a grandmother just last week."

"I've been here 15 years, and I don't recall a case where someone tried to get a weapon in. But then, the metal detector would pick that up. The metal detector doesn't pick up drugs, and that's mostly what we have problems with. In addition to the ones we arrest, we suspend visits to another 15 or 20 a month because we have reasonable cause to suspect that they're going to try something."

A younger officer who has been assigned to the visiting room on several occasions feels that "Maybe 20 percent are legitimate visits. Parents coming to see their son. A wife whose husband got caught up in a bad situation, and he's not really a bad convict. But from what I've dealt with, I still see some sort of a racket going on. There's still some sort of connection going on. Eighty percent are still scheming.

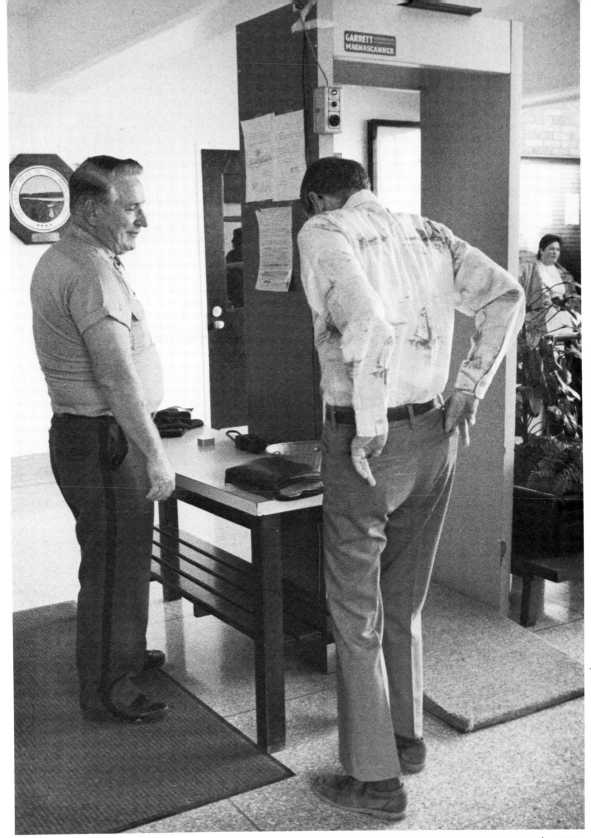

METAL DETECTOR: *Visitors must empty all of their pockets and pass through a metal detector before entering the visiting room or any other part of the prison.*

"But it does get very emotional with those who are here for true visits. A wife crying. A child waving goodbye to her daddy. But you have to be security minded.

"After visiting hours are over, we make a search of the whole area. It's a thorough search. You go through the seams of the draperies, you go up under the heater ducts, you lift your arm up under the Coke dispenser."

Not every inmate has frequent visitors. For some, the friends or relatives live too far away to visit more than once or twice a year. For others, visiting hours are not necessarily pleasant experiences.

"I don't have many visits," says one. "And that's good. Because I usually find out that they got more problems than I do."

Another inmate, who is older and serving a long sentence, says, "Visits can help a lot for these younger guys, but they got to remember not to get all riled up (sexually aroused) when they're out there. They get all riled up, then they come back inside here, and it just makes it worse."

FAMILY CARD GAME: Inmates are allowed two visits per month from each family member.

Opposite Page—*MAN WITH CHILD: For many inmates, visiting hours are what keeps them going from week to week.*

INMATE AND PARENTS: Lebanon inmates are permitted to have up to four visitors at a time. In addition to family members, inmates are allowed to have two friends on their approved visitors list.

THE COUPLE: *In addition to the visiting room, there are picnic tables outside where inmates can gather with family and friends.*

Opposite Page—PHOTO BACKDROP: *The visiting room has a scenic backdrop where inmates and guests can have their picture taken.*

INMATE AND WIFE: *Visits are important to the inmates, but they also provide security problems for the officers. The officers try to keep their distance, but must keep a close eye to make sure contraband is not smuggled into the prison.*

8

Economics 101

"Howard" has served 11 years on a murder charge of 15 years to life. He served eight years at two other institutions, first in a maximum, then in a minimum security prison. A "knife charge and a drug charge" upgraded his status to Lebanon's close security three years ago. He makes $17 a month from his job and has no outside source of income. He maintains that he cannot make it on that amount of money and that he must supplement his income in other ways.

"At one time you could get packages," he says. "Your soap, shampoo, deodorant. Personal hygiene stuff. Well, they stopped that. Now you got to buy it out of the commissary.

"I gamble. I play football. You know, bet on football pools. A hustle here and there. Before I got caught, I was making about $80 a month stealing out of food service. But they put a stop to that."

Howard also admits to running a store. That is, he purchases items from the commissary, then resells on credit to inmates who are temporarily broke. The standard rate is two for one from state day to state day (paydays). If the borrower does not meet his obligation in time, the rate can then double or triple.

Howard maintains that he does not use strongarm tactics to collect and that he simply avoids selling goods to deadbeats. But not all store owners operate that way. Some will collect their debts by forcing the borrower into sexual acts, having them do their work for them, or running dope deals.

One inmate admitted that the inmate stores were good places to stay away from, but also admired the store owners. "They are businessmen. You gotta respect that."

Prison officials discourage the stores, and those who are caught are charged with a major violation.

THE CLERK: *This inmate works as a clerk for some of the officers.*

"We have rules on how much of certain items you can have in your cell," says a senior officer. "Especially cigarettes, which is the equivalent of cash money in here. But they'll find ways around it. They'll have their cellie say it's his, or they'll spread it around among their friends. We usually catch them when someone gets in over his head and snitches, or we'll find the set of books they keep. They can't keep all that information in their heads—they have to write it down."

The officers maintain that inmates can get by on their salaries. Everyone is required to work, and the wages range from $17 to over $100 a month, depending on the inmate's job. The state provides toiletries and bulk tobacco for those who cannot afford to purchase brand names in the commissary. But the inmates complain that the state products are inferior, so the stores and the hustles remain an entrenched way of life at Lebanon.

Inmates with "talent"—those who can draw or paint or make jewelry boxes out of match sticks or model cars out of paper—often sell the items to supplement their incomes. Others resort to dealing drugs.

"You can get anything you want in here for a pack of cigarettes," says one inmate. Adds another, "This is just another city inside a fence. You have everything. You can gamble, you can get your homosexuals, you can play the numbers. Anything."

Some inmates have other jobs that can help them supplement their income. One inmate says he gets better haircuts at the prison barbershop by rewarding the barber with two packs of cigarettes. Another tells of getting extra clothes, and a third maintains he makes a little extra by pressing clothes.

"The inmates," explains an officer, "are not paid in money—money is illegal in here—but their wages are credited to their accounts each month. So cigarettes become the unit of exchange. We have rules on trading and that sort of thing. The dealing is done in the blocks. We watch out for it, and we do a pretty good job of controlling it, but we can't totally prevent it."

Many officers have difficulty mustering sympathy for the inmate who gets in over his head through gambling or running up a debt at a store. "I don't have any sympathy for a guy who won't pay his bills," says one officer. "Besides, there's really no reason for them to get into that stuff."

In one way or another, however, the underground economy flourishes at Lebanon, and the economic status of the inmates is evident if one knows what to look for. Towels are the big status symbol and are used to decorate the cells. The inmates make bedspreads, pillow covers, rugs, and tablecloths from them.

The physical appearance of the inmate is another measure. Some have civilian clothes to supplement their state issue. Others have tailored pants and several extra changes of clothes.

Says one inmate, "I've got my work clothes, and I have clothes I go to the dining room in, and clothes for recreation, and clothes that I visit my family in. I try to maintain a good appearance."

Some inmates do well economically because they have family or friends who send them money periodically, and the money is credited to their accounts. For some, especially those who are considered weak, it is the extra money that prevents them from getting "turned out" or becoming involved with the more dangerous elements inside the prison.

THE LAUNDRY ROOM: Two thousand inmates provide these two men with ample work each week.

ELECTRICAL SHOP: This inmate works in the electrical shop at Lebanon, repairing prison property.

Opposite Page—*KITCHEN DUTY: Six thousand meals a day are prepared at Lebanon. Inmates on kitchen duty are closely supervised because of the potential to turn normal kitchenware into weapons.* ———→

THE COMMISSARY: *The prison commissary sells soda, snacks, cigarettes, and coffee. In addition, most inmates choose to purchase brand name soap, deodorant, and toothpaste rather than use the state-issued products.*

Opposite Page—INMATE WITH GROCERIES: *Inmates are allowed to go to the commissary once a week. The most sought after items are cigarettes and coffee.* ⟶

THE TAG SHOP: *All of Ohio's license plates are made at Lebanon.*

Somebody's Children

While it would be convenient to sum up life at the Lebanon Correctional Institution with a few well-chosen stereotypes, it's not that easy. Like the society that surrounds it, prison life is a varied, complex, and often contradictory environment.

The inmates come from every walk of life. Some were reared in prosperous, upper-middle-class surroundings, while others have spent their lives in abject poverty. Some are talented and educated, while others get by on their wits or through brute strength. Some are serving their first sentence, while others are repeat offenders who have spent most of their adult lives behind bars.

There are basically two codes of conduct. One is handed down by prison officials in the form of written documents; the other is a series of unspoken rules and regulations developed by the inmates themselves.

While it is obvious that many inmates use the rehabilitation programs in an attempt to improve their lives, it is equally obvious that others see those programs as a scam they must go through to impress the parole board. There are inmates who live in fear, and there are inmates who prey on the weakest of their peers. Some inmates count with precision-like accuracy the days until their release or next parole hearing. Others have become fully institutionalized and readily accept the fact that their release may never come.

In some respects, prison life seems tame. It is a controlled environment where, statistically, there is probably less violence than is found in a typical American community of equal size. On the other hand, it takes only a few hours before even the most callous visitor begins to feel his senses sharpening and adopts some of the same cautiousness displayed by inmates and officers alike.

To the disinterested observer, the rules and regulations enforced by the officers are easy to understand. But it is also easy to understand the loneliness, fears, tension, and frustration of the inmates. It is impossible to forget that they are in prison because they committed crimes against—and posed a threat to—society. It is equally impossible to forget the tortured expressions of the families during visits or the defeated look on an inmate's face after he has been "turned out."

Perhaps the best summary came from Grace Wojda after she had finished photographing the prison.

"During each of my visits, I asked the officers and inmates to avoid discussing the kind of crime anyone had committed. I didn't want to know what anyone was in for or how long of a sentence he was serving.

"As a photographer, I had to stay totally neutral. My job was to capture the images of the prison as objectively as I could. I wanted to produce a straight documentary, without taking sides.

"But as a mother, I could not help but think that at one time all of these men were somebody's children, innocent and uncorrupted and with a bright future in front of them. And I could not help but ask myself what went wrong that they ended up in here."

BEHIND BARS

An Album

A SUMMER AFTERNOON: Both inmates and officers agree that the summer months run more smoothly because the inmates have more time to enjoy recreation privileges outside.

THE WATERING TROUGH: An inmate stops for a drink to help ward off the hot afternoon sun.

INMATE WITH BABY: An inmate gets his first chance to be with his newborn baby.

INSIDE A CELL: Inmates must purchase their own televisions, radios, and fans. An inmate's wealth is partially revealed by the number of towels he has. Towels are used to drape over furnishings, make pillow covers, and otherwise decorate the cell.

Opposite Page—*MAXIMUM SECURITY INMATE: Maximum security cells are not permitted many of the luxuries afforded other cell blocks and the environment is rather spartan.*

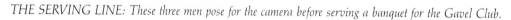

THE SERVING LINE: These three men pose for the camera before serving a banquet for the Gavel Club.

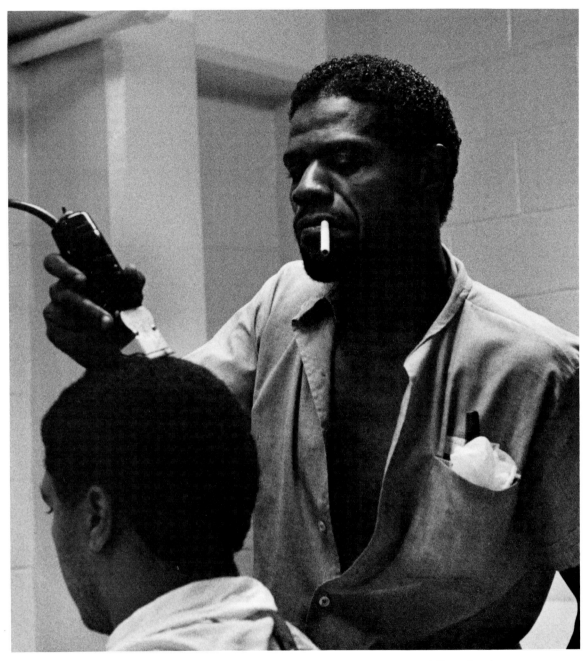

PRISON BARBERSHOP: Lebanon's barbershop is staffed by inmates who learn their skills on the job.

Opposite Page—A REFRESHING PAUSE: This inmate is obviously enjoying his cigarette break. The prison provides bulk tobacco for those who cannot afford to purchase cigarettes in the commissary.

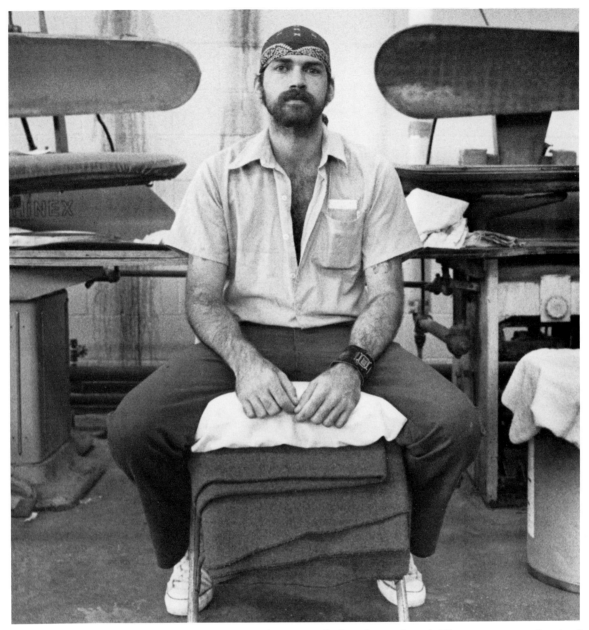

TAKING A BREAK: Inmates earn between $17 and $100 a month, depending on their job. This inmate operates the prison's ironing tables.

Opposite Page—*THE TOOL MAN: This inmate works in the prison's machine shop.*

Page 90—*THE ILLUSTRATED MAN: This inmate takes pride in his tattoos and his weight-lifting abilities. He has won several trophies for the latter.*

Page 91—*PRIDE: Many inmates take a lot of pride in their appearance. Prison rules dictate that shirts must be tucked in whenever an inmate leaves his cell.*

About the Photographer

Grace L. Wojda is a photojournalist from Wilmington, Ohio. Her photos have appeared in *Homeless in America* and *Government in America,* as well as in many newspapers and magazines. She was a participating photographer in the Homeless in America exhibit, which toured 32 American cities and won her the 1988 Leica Medal of Excellence Award for photojournalism. Her exhibit of the Lebanon Correctional Institution is currently on tour and earned her a major award from the National University Continuing Education Association. She is an honors graduate of Treasure Valley Community College and attended Boise State University.

About the Authors

Raymond G. Wojda has been a public relations practitioner for the past 15 years and has received marketing and advertising awards from the Public Relations Society of America, the American Marketing Association, and the National Council for the Advancement and Support of Education. An honors graduate of the University of Michigan, he is a former newspaper reporter and magazine editor whose articles have appeared in numerous publications.

Norman Erik Smith is the Vice President for Academic Affairs at Wilmington College in Wilmington, Ohio. He coordinated the college's educational programs at several Ohio prisons for 12 years and has published several scholarly works on prison inmates. He is currently completing work on a new model of social interaction among inmates. He is an honors graduate of the University of Bridgeport and received his Ph.D. from Ohio State University.

Richard K. Jones is the senior correctional officer at the Lebanon Correctional Institution in Lebanon, Ohio. He has been involved in corrections for 16 years and has worked in all areas of prison operations. He is a graduate of Wilmington College and received his M.S. degree in criminal justice from Xavier University.